The Spy
on Noah's Ark

and Other Bible Stories
from the Inside Out

by Lindsay Hardin Freeman

The Spy
on Noah's Ark

and Other Bible Stories
from the Inside Out

by Lindsay Hardin Freeman
Illustrations by Paul Shaffer
Leonard Freeman, Story Collaborator

Forward Movement
Cincinnati, Ohio

Illustrations by Paul Shaffer

Book design by Carole Miller

© 2013 by Forward Movement

All rights reserved.

ISBN 978-0-88028-365-6

Printed in USA

Library of Congress Cataloging-in-Publication Data

Freeman, Lindsay Hardin.
   The spy on Noah's ark : and other Bible stories from the inside out /by Lindsay Hardin Freeman ; artwork by Paul Shaffer ; Leonard Freeman, story collaborator.
      pages cm
   Summary: Relates stories from the Bible from the perspective of a dove on the ark, David's slingshot, the star of Bethlehem, and more. Includes discussion questions for adults and children.
   ISBN 978-0-88028-365-6
   1. Bible stories, English. I. Shaffer, Paul (Clergyman), illustrator. II. Freeman, Leonard W. III. Title.
   BS551.3.F743 2013
   220.95'05--dc23
                              2013021680

Forward Movement
412 Sycamore Street
Cincinnati, Ohio 45202
+1 800 543 1813
www.forwardmovement.org

Dedicated to

David, Jeffrey, Daniel, Matthew,
Kate, and Michael Freeman

and the people of
St. Jude's Episcopal Mission
Ocean View, Hawaii

What Readers Are Saying...

This book has lots of animals and I like it. I can read most of it myself!

— RACHEL E. A. HOLBROOK, AGE 7
ST. MARK'S EPISCOPAL SCHOOL
UPLAND, CALIFORNIA

༄ ༄ ༄

I liked the dove and the Federal Birds of Investigation. Also I liked how it was taken from the dove and the other animals' perspective in a way I could understand. Definitely a thumbs up!'

— ALEX HAMANN, AGE 10
WILMINGTON, NORTH CAROLINA

༄ ༄ ༄

Lindsay Hardin Freeman's retellings of old favorite Bible stories pop with life—slugs and sloths, slurping and slithering. Concrete and whimsical details told by her animal and object narrators make you want to read these stories out loud to the nearest children you can find. This collection wonderfully celebrates creation!

— THE VERY REV. CYNTHIA BRIGGS KITTREDGE
DEAN AND PRESIDENT
PROFESSOR OF NEW TESTAMENT
SEMINARY OF THE SOUTHWEST
AUSTIN, TEXAS

༄ ༄ ༄

With humor, wit, and a special skill that draws the reader into her narrative, the author retells a number of traditional Bible stories from unexpected perspectives—a delightful way for people of all ages and religious backgrounds to acquaint or reacquaint themselves with these important writings.

— ANNE MCKINNON
CIVIC ACTIVIST
NEWTON, MASSACHUSETTS

༄ ༄ ༄

Talented author Lindsay Hardin Freeman, who in The Scarlet Cord *creatively breathed new life into the stories of women of the Bible, has once again stirred our imagination in* The Spy on Noah's Ark and Other Bible Stories from the Inside Out. *A wonderful read for all ages, Freeman takes classic biblical narratives and provides a new perspective.*

— THE RT. REV. BRIAN N. PRIOR
BISHOP, THE EPISCOPAL CHURCH IN MINNESOTA
MINNEAPOLIS, MINNESOTA

This wonderful book is an opportunity for young people and adults to read favorite stories anew and to gain fresh perspectives on the characters. It is a valuable resource for families and congregations.

THE REV. DR. SHERYL A. KUJAWA-HOLBROOK
CLAREMONT SCHOOL OF THEOLOGY
BLOY HOUSE, THE EPISCOPAL SCHOOL OF THEOLOGY AT CLAREMONT
CLAREMONT, CALIFORNIA

The Spy *is filled with imaginative and beautifully crafted narrations of biblical stories in which previously silent eyewitnesses recount God's love for us and his saving actions in times of danger. I can't wait to read these stories to my grandchildren and watch how they respond.*

—ROBERT LARNER
LECTOR AND SCRIPTURE STUDY GROUP FACILITATOR
ST. BERNARD'S ROMAN CATHOLIC PARISH
NEWTON, MASSACHUSETTS

These creative and playful reimaginations of familiar Bible stories are full of sounds, smells, and sights that will stir up a child's own creative thinking. Questions and comments at the end of each story encourage further reflection for both children and adults. A great resource for parishes and families!

—THE REV. CLARE FISCHER-DAVIS
RECTOR, ST. MARTIN'S EPISCOPAL CHURCH
PROVIDENCE, RHODE ISLAND

Refreshing, beautiful, inspiring, and creative—these are all words I would use to describe the first-person narrative writings of Lindsay Hardin Freeman. Children (and adults too) reading this new work will find themselves inside the stories, feeling in the center of centuries-old accounts of God's relationship with and love for his creation, all creation. This in turn could spur readers to begin their own journey of faith with the Living God.

—JULIE H. CRIDER
BOOK GROUP FACILITATOR
DAMARISCOTTA BAPTIST CHURCH
DAMARISCOTTA, MAINE

Brilliant words and pictures bring Bible stories to life in a way that children, parents, and grandparents will enjoy. I look forward to reading it to my own great-grandchildren!

— CORDELIA BURT
ST. JUDE'S EPISCOPAL MISSION
OCEAN VIEW, HAWAII

In The Spy on Noah's Ark, *treasured Bible stories come alive through the most unlikely of characters. These "eyewitnesses" to God's wonders open the way to a great time of sharing and discussion for all.*

— KATHY AND LARRY WELLIVER
MESSIAH UNITED METHODIST CHURCH
PLYMOUTH, MINNESOTA

The Rev. Lindsay Hardin Freeman has a special gift of finding the hidden treasure in the Bible and weaving it into exciting and grace-filled stories. This book is surely the living proof of her gift, and I recommend it to all who are thirsty for really cool Bible stories for their children as well as themselves.

— JISOOK PAIK, PhD
VISITING SCHOLAR AND PROFESSOR
UNIVERSITY OF NORTH FLORIDA

As a storyteller, I appreciated reading and reflecting on the biblical stories as told by Lindsay Hardin Freeman. I can easily imagine adapting these tales for oral storytelling events to the delight of children and adults alike. Conversations following the events will come alive with the help of the excellent questions accompanying each story.

— The Rt. Rev. Michael Hanley
Episcopal Bishop of Oregon
Portland, Oregon

✿ ❧ ✿

Here in Kenya, where we work with unwed teenage moms as young as 12, stories from The Spy on Noah's Ark *assist them in learning the foundations of the Christian faith and give them joy and laughter in a challenging world. Reading the stories and experiencing the art helps them to cross cultural, historical, and theological boundaries. Their children will soon be second-generation readers of this wonderful book!*

— Carol Erickson
Executive Director
Imara International
Nanyuki, Kenya

✿ ❧ ✿

Mothers, grandmothers, teachers, and caregivers can find here stories to pass on to future women, and men, of faith. It is a delight to have Lindsay Hardin Freeman share these stories from her days as a young mother and nurturer.

— The Rev. Deacon Nancy R. Crawford
National President, Episcopal Church Women
Eugene, Oregon

✿ ❧ ✿

The first step in learning ethical behavior is being able to see things from the other point of view. Even if parents or godparents are not theatrically inclined, all they have to do is read and watch what the animals say and voila—instant and engaging authenticity!

— Roxanne Ezell
Plymouth Congregational Church
— The Rev. Dr. Roger Ezell
Presbytery of the Twin Cities
Minneapolis, Minnesota

✿ ❧ ✿

Contents

If they could talk...

If you are a child reading this book, you are a good reader. And if you are a parent or grandparent reading it with a child, you are blessed to have a young one with whom to explore God's Word. Those little people know a lot more than we think. They're much closer to God's breath in creation than are we; they've most recently had God's hand move over them as they came into being.

Sometimes, whether young or old, it's tempting to think that we're the only ones who know about God. Before God got around to making people, though, God started with light and dark and rocks and trees and animals and insects.

And those parts of creation, just like us, would have much to say about God if they could talk. Witness in this book God's hand at work in the world about us, spoken by voices that have kept quiet for centuries. See the stories of the Bible from the inside out. Creatures, angels, and stars tell of their experiences with God, their discoveries, and, most of all, their joys.

☙ ❧ ☙

Please visit
www.forwardmovementkids.org
for coloring pages for *The Spy on Noah's Ark*
and to see our other children's materials.

Introduction and Acknowledgements

It is hard to tell God's story when we are not confident of our own biblical fluency. In a world where our children are surrounded by technology, sports, music lessons, and what seems like too much homework and not enough play time, the Bible often gets relegated to Sunday morning, or worse— dismissed. And that is a profound loss.

Some things are not essential. Bible stories are. If our children do not learn the great lessons of our faith, they stand on shakier ground and have fewer moral compass points from which to draw. If they believe that we do not care about scripture, they will find it hard to care about it as well.

Facing the deep challenges of life, as we all do, is hard enough. It is even harder when there is little reservoir of faith or knowledge of how our spiritual ancestors triumphed over similar times of stress and agony.

So, take your children to church. Read Bible stories to your grandchildren. Ask them how they see God. Plant the seeds now for a lifetime of faith.

This book, twenty years in the making, is meant to help with that process, drawing from all of God's creation to help both children and adults see God's actions in a new light.

✍ ⚜ ✍

Many thanks to Forward Movement, especially the Rev. Scott Gunn and Richelle Thompson for their vision and commitment to The Episcopal Church and readers of all ages, and to Janet Buening and Carole Miller for their unending support, fine tuning, and graceful suggestions.

Thank you to the Rev. Paul Shaffer, whose brilliant artwork will make even the crankiest Christian smile and think. Thank you to Jeffrey and David Freeman, who grew up on these stories and offered humorous suggestions. Thank you to Katherine Boyle for her grace and skill and to Roxanne Ezell for her eagle eye.

Thank you to the children at St. Martin's-by-the-Lake Episcopal Church in Minnetonka Beach, Minnesota, who provided an enthusiastic laboratory in which we could test the stories. And "mahalo" to the people of St. Jude's Episcopal Mission, Ocean View, Hawaii, for giving us a sanctuary in which to finish this book.

I am particularly grateful to my husband, the Rev. Leonard Freeman, for his "finish carpentry" work, creative spark, and faithful insights. Without him, the joie de vivre would be missing, both in this book and in my life.

Most of the direct Bible quotes are from a dynamic and gracious resource, *The Message/Remix, The Bible in Contemporary Language*, by Eugene H. Peterson. The remaining quotes are paraphrased from standard Bible texts.

— THE REV. LINDSAY HARDIN FREEMAN

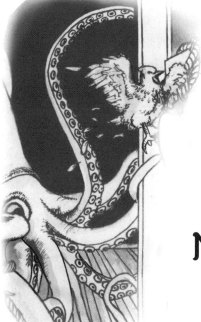

Chapter 1

The Spy on Noah's Ark

by the Dove

D o you know the story of Noah's ark? Animals, two by two, boarded a big boat that Noah built and sailed away. The rest of the world flooded, but Noah and his family and the animals were safe. And I was there. I was one of the two doves on board.

I can just hear you now. *So what?* you say. *A bird. A boat. A flood. Big deal.*

Little do you know. You see, I have a secret that I've never told anyone until now.

I was a spy, working for God as a special agent on Noah's ark. I am, in fact, the first dove to have served in the FBI: The Federal Birds of Investigation. And my job was important. I was assigned to watch all of the ark's passengers and to tell God if they needed anything. Boats are strange places, after all. How odd it feels if you have hooves and are used to soft grass underfoot, or if you have lived deep in the ground and suddenly you are on a world that rocks and moves and sloshes! God told me to comfort the animals and remind them that they were safe in his hands.

God had created the world hoping that people would be kind to each other and that all living creatures would get along. But peace did not last. People started doing bad things. Bullying, killing, stealing, you name it. Trouble was everywhere.

With a heartbreaking sigh, God made a tough decision to start the world over again. He told a good man named Noah to gather his family and two of every living thing, and to build a ship for all of them to sail on, because God was going to send a flood.

When the ark was only a plan in Noah's mind, breezes were fresh and warm, and the sky was blue with nothing but puffy white clouds. Noah gathered wood until his yard was a mountain of logs. Then, without a word, he and his family started building.

— — —

As the months went by, the sky became dark and angry. *Crash! Boom! Rumble! Bumble!* Thunder and lightning raged. Rain pounded the ground. With the water rising around him, Noah built that ark higher and higher, with giant stalls for big animals and tiny cubbyholes for little ones. At last a huge boat stood before him, longer than a football field and as tall as a four-story building!

Would the boat float? Noah wasn't a builder by trade, so it was hard to tell. But after one particularly dark night, God's voice boomed from the clouds: "IT IS TIME!" The animals then came running, squawking, squeaking, and mooing, slithering, flying, hooting and hissing, dancing and prancing, squiggling and slurping, male and female, two by two, onto the great ark.

Worms wriggled up out of the ground. Tigers bounded, roaring out of the woods. With a "Skree, skree!" hawks dove from the sky. "Tahoot, tahoot! Don't forget us," called the owls. "Snork, snork, we are here," grunted the pigs.

Tree sloths never moved so fast as they did with acorn-sized hail blinging down on their backs. It was a grand sight, with pairs of every animal on earth rushing on board. You never see cockroaches or slugs or snakes in ark pictures, but they were there, too. God didn't forget anyone.

There were so many of us that it took all day to board the ark. Scuffles broke out between a few—like the wolves who thought the coyotes had a better view of the moon—but soon everyone was cozy-comfortable in their new homes. Bedtime stories brayed by the donkeys made us laugh. Frogs chanting lullabies made us drowsy. As the fireflies lighted the dusk, we drifted off to sleep...until the giant boat, lurching and pitching, rose up and left the land behind.

In the morning we watched the lands and homes of our world disappear. Shrubs first, then treetops and meadows. As the waters rose, whole towns vanished, their tiled roofs disappearing under the waves. Not a single living thing was to be seen above the great flood. It brought a tear to my eye. Yet I had to trust that God had a glorious vision for a new world.

My work started quickly. "It's okay, little friend," I sang to a trembling mouse, "God will not let you drown."

"Coo, coo, Mrs. Elephant," I chanted, perched on her wavering trunk. "Noah has plenty of fresh straw for you, don't you worry, don't worry."

Squeak, holler, moo. Most of us had never been away from our homes before. It was a little scary.

⟋⟍ ⟅⟆ ⟋⟍

We sailed and sailed, for days upon days upon days. Some counted forty days and nights on board. Others counted months and months. We rode high on those waves, not seeing anything but water and sky and each other. And it wasn't the pleasure cruise that you might think.

Every night, just as the roosters and elephants were going to bed, the owls would wake up, all wide-eyed and screechy. Just as the lambs ventured out for their morning stroll, the boa constrictors unwound, making the woolly little creatures scramble and run for cover.

What would *you* do locked up for so long? The moose took cats and dogs for rides on their antlers, and the serpents chased things they'd never seen before, like peacocks with sparkling tails.

You should have seen the giant squids poking out their huge tentacles, trying to catch the chickens. They didn't want to hurt anyone. They were just having fun with all of their arms.

The rain continued to pound away. Lightning, thunder, hail. *Crash, Bam, Bingle, Boom!* You name it, we heard it. That doesn't count the groans and creaks of the ark itself as waves pushed and pulled at us, whirling and swirling, often flinging us side to side. A wild ride for all of us, until we found our sea legs—and our sea wings, tails, and fins! Even though the ark continued to crack and shudder, it became a trusted friend.

And then one night—*bump, scrape, bam*—our ark bumped into something, something we hadn't felt in forever. Something solid. Mountain-top rocks. "Rummmpphhh!" bellowed the bears from below, angry and hungry from months of hibernation. "Squawwwkkkkkk!" went the geese. "What is this, matey? What is this, matey?" yelled parrots from the third floor. "Moooomy!" bellowed the cows. "Snnnoooorrrrkkkkk?" asked the pigs.

Then came the sound of a door creaking open from the family rooms. Noah stepped out, nightcap on head, candle in hand. Starting at the bottom of the ark, he hummed to the llamas, petted the dogs, threw a ball for the wolves, scratched the pigs, and cheeped to the sparrows.

Finally he reached our cage and gently pushed in his arm. "Step up little one, come on out. We have things to do, you and I."

Hopping up on his wrist, I waited while he stroked my head, neck, and pin feathers. After all the storms, it was so soothing. "Leave your nest, little one," he said. "Go out and see what green places you can find. We are all ready to leave this boat."

Noah opened a tiny window, motioning me to go. I pushed against his hand, stretched my wings, and flew out. Immediately I remembered the joy of wind through my feathers. Up and down I sailed, basking in the fresh air and the light of the rising sun.

Sadly, there was no land to be seen. I flew back to the ark and reported that we were still stranded. Noah's eyes dimmed and he walked away, muttering that he would talk with God.

The animals were strangely quiet. Only the mournful howl of a homesick coyote broke the silence.

⟳ ⟰ ⟳

Seven days later later Noah asked me to try again. Still no land in sight, yet this time I found a floating green olive branch and carried it back. Waving it over his head, Noah danced a little jig, shouting, "Yes, Yes!" as he carried it through the boat, splashing drops of water over the goats and sheep and horses who baaed and raahhed and stamped their feet in delight. Hope was in the air.

Finally, several days later, I flew out again and returned with the joyous news. "Land, ho! It's right over there! Lush rain forests, soothing waterfalls, high trees for making new homes, COO, COO, COO!"

The ark pitched up and down—this time not from the waves, but from all of the happy feet. *Woof! Skree! Caw! Ko-kie! Hahoo, hahoo!* As the gangplank lowered, everybody—animals, fish, birds, people—cried their delight. The beach filled with the joyous sound of crowing, barking, hooting, squawking, and singing. Monkeys did cartwheels on the sand, cockroaches skittered toward wet logs, bats flew up like playing cards tossed into the sky. We had made it! A new world to begin!

And begin it did. Within months, we were raising families, including my honey dove and me. Every so often you'd see a dog asking for a ride on the moose's antlers, or a squid swooping up to the ocean's surface to wave a tentacle. We'd learned an important lesson—that all of us in creation are bound together in one big story.

Now that the world had a new start, God promised never to flood it again. Marking that promise was a big beautiful rainbow in the sky. The next time you see a rainbow, look a little closer—Federal Birds of Investigation at your service. I'm flying right over the top.

❧ ❧ ❧

From the Bible

God continued, "This is the sign of the covenant I am making between me and you and everything living around you and everyone living after you. I'm putting my rainbow in the clouds, a sign of the covenant between me and the Earth. From now on, when I form a cloud over the Earth and the rainbow appears in the cloud, I'll remember my covenant between me and you and everything living, that never again will floodwaters destroy all life."

— GENESIS 9:12-15

❧ ❧ ❧

For Children

- Why did God save Noah and his family?

- What do you think it must have been like to be cooped up in the ark for so long?

- What do you think it was like for the ark's passengers to see that rainbow? What does that rainbow mean to you?

- The animals and birds and fish were different from each other. Do you live or work or go to school with people who are different? What can you learn from the story of Noah's ark?

For Adults

God tells Noah that he must change his life to survive—and he does. He quits his day job (presumably) and starts building the ark; he ensures his family is on board; he protects God's creation. He does not shirk from listening to God, and he is able to rise above the likely negativity of friends and colleagues.

What might God be saying to you about the direction of your life? Is it time to forge a new path? To lead others to a life-giving destination? To care for a different part of God's world? Noah constructed an ark and set sail: What steps might you take to respond to God's stirrings in your heart?

Chapter 2

Jonah: The Passenger in My Stomach

by the Whale

I am a whale, a big gray whale, and I live in the Mediterranean Sea. One day I swallowed up a man named Jonah. He tasted terrible and wasn't worth the trouble. Jonah must have been special, though, because God came looking for him and I had to spit him out. I've been famous ever since. When you hear people say, "Jonah in the belly of the whale," that's my belly they are talking about.

The day I ate him, the sea was restless, tossing the fishing boats around like toys. Most storms brew for hours, but this one came up within minutes. The blue sky turned black, and the gentle breezes suddenly blew furiously. From one particular boat, rolling up and down the waves like a yo-yo on a string, I could hear tense and angry voices arguing.

Curious, I swam closer. If they needed help ending their argument, just a flip of my tail would send them splashing into the sea. Yet I'm a softie. I just wanted to listen.

"This storm is a nightmare!" one sailor yelled.

"Why is this happening? God, save us!" pleaded another.

As their voices grew muffled, I knew they had gone below deck to seek shelter from the whipping rain.

"This must be your fault," they accused someone. "You're the reason we're all going to drown. What have you done to make God angry?"

Then I heard the voice of the man named Jonah.

"You are right, this storm is my fault. God asked me to do something, and instead I ran away. I thought if I sailed away, I would not have to obey God. I was wrong.

"God asked me to journey to Nineveh, a city that is full of hard-hearted people, to tell them that he exists. If they know about him, they can change their ways. He can save them. But I'm scared they will hurt me. You see, my name, Jonah, means 'dove,' and we doves always fly away from bad people, not toward them. That's why I'm here, not there!"

The waves grew higher, tossing the boat.

"See? God is angry with me for running away. If you get rid of me, the water will calm down," said Jonah.

"We must do what he says!" cried a sailor.

"What's there to lose?" yelled another above the roar of the sea.

Next thing I knew, a scrawny little guy came flying out of the boat, smack down into the water, headfirst. Well, I know a good lunch when I see one. So I swallowed him up, in one big gulp. Within minutes, the sea calmed down, and the little boat sailed peacefully homeward.

◌ ◌ ◌

Jonah was a little strange. He was not a normal meal in my belly. Normal meals don't talk to themselves. For three days I could feel him walking around in my stomach, and I could hear his voice rumbling up from inside me. "God, save me! God, save me! I don't want to die! You have my attention. I will do what you want!"

We whales are a very ancient race. We have heard the voice of God within our waters for eons and ages, guiding us in the ways of life. So when on the third night the Voice came, I knew, and I obeyed.

"BRING HIM FORTH!" it said.

With a deep breath and a flip of my tail, I spit Jonah right out onto the beach nearest Nineveh. He was slimy but alive, and very, very grateful.

The adventure was still not finished. Unbeknownst to me, Jonah's time with me was the talk of the ocean. Surfacing to blow through my spout one fine morning, I heard some seagulls chattering about my lost meal.

"Jonah learned a lesson," cawed one bird as she cruised overhead. "Next time, he'll do what God wants him to do instead of running away!"

"He's not the only one who learned something," cawed another. "Those people in Nineveh changed their ways when they heard him speak. He told them to love God, and now they do!"

Amazing. The scrawny little guy did what God asked and everything changed, including him.

I hope to see Jonah again someday, but next time I will not swallow him.

In the meantime, me?

I just keep swimming the seas, looking for my next good meal.

꧁ ꙮ ꧂

From the Bible

Jonah prayed: "In trouble, deep trouble, I prayed to GOD." He answered me. From the belly of the grave I cried, 'Help!' You heard my cry."

— JONAH 2:1-2

꧁ ꙮ ꧂

For Children

- Jonah ran away instead of saying yes to God. Have you ever not done something you've been asked to do? How did you feel?

- Do you think God was glad to hear from Jonah when he cried out for help? Why?

- What does this story say about trusting in God?

For Adults

Have you, like Jonah, ever been swallowed up, crushed under the weight of responsibilities, insecurities, or fear? Trapped in the belly of the whale, Jonah cried out to God for help. Humbled, he found it—and was able to walk freely in God's light, committed to new work. What darkness and trouble might you name and ask God to deliver you from?

Chapter 3

The Baby in the Bulrushes

by the Bullfrog

Have you ever seen a bulrush? That's a strange name, isn't it? My name is almost the same—I'm a bullfrog. Perhaps you've heard that opposites attract? Well, we are about as opposite as we could be. Bulrushes are plants. Straight and slim, they can grow taller than a person. Short and squat and noisy best describes us bullfrogs, yet we live in harmony with our plant neighbors. Even though we are different, the bullrushes and bullfrogs worked together thousands of years ago to save someone important.

The river where we live is the Nile, the longest river in the world, flowing through Africa and Egypt. And the person we saved was Moses, the famous Hebrew leader, when he was just a little baby. At night when we croak lullabies to our little ones, we most often tell this story, for it is the one they like best of all.

Close your eyes now. Pretend you were with us that morning as we woke to the footsteps of a young woman, racing down to the water, looking this way and that, out of breath.

She carried a beautiful woven basket. Placing the basket deep in the reedy bulrushes so that no one could see it, she laid her head on it, kissed it, and whispered, "Take care of him, God. I love him so much. Please keep him safe." Then she ran back up the bank and disappeared.

✍ ✧ ✍

Like hula dancers gracefully waving their arms to and fro, the bulrushes rocked the basket back and forth, back and forth. We sang comforting songs—*garump, garump*—to help whomever was inside to not be scared. As the sun grew hotter, the bulrushes draped themselves over the basket to provide shelter and shade.

Soon there was a commotion on the beach. The ruler of our land was called Pharaoh, and we could see his daughter approaching, surrounded by servants carrying towels and soap and containers of sweet fragrances. She was going to take a bath in the river.

She waded in, not far from where we stood, laughing and scooping up water, her long dark hair glistening in the sun. But then we froze, because we all heard something. From the basket came the sound of crying!

Pharaoh's daughter glanced over at us, tossed her hair, and went back to washing.

Then it happened again: crying—long, deep, wrenching sounds. We GARUMPED as loudly as we could to cover up the wailing. Yet Pharaoh's daughter trampled right over us, found the basket, and flipped it open.

And then she saw the baby. He was a beautiful dark-haired child about three months old, his face red and swollen from crying. He must have missed his mother as much as she missed him.

Pharaoh's daughter looked deep into the child's eyes and lifted him to her shoulder. He snuggled in like a kitten, and his tears stopped.

"This is a Hebrew baby," she said. "His mother must be hiding him to save his life."

✿ ✿ ✿

We shivered as we heard those words, our voices growing faint. Pharaoh had kept the Hebrew people as slaves for centuries. He starved them, worked them harder each year, and never gave them a day off. You would think they would grow weaker and weaker, but each year their bodies grew more muscular and their numbers grew larger. Unlike Pharaoh, the Hebrew people believed in God.

They became so strong in body and spirit that Pharaoh feared they would overthrow him. So he made a horrible law. He declared that all the Hebrew boy babies must be killed so that they could not grow up to take his place. Because of this dreadful law, no Hebrew boy baby was safe.

Back at the river, all time seemed to stop as Pharaoh's daughter pondered the fate of the child in her arms. We frogs sat at full attention, wide-eyed on our lily pads. The bulrushes held themselves tight in the wind.

If the baby was worried, he wasn't showing it. Clenching her long hair in his tiny hands, he twisted it, watching it catch the sunlight over the river. Seeing that, we sang loudly together, serenading the young woman as she considered what to do. In that happy moment, a bond formed between them, one that would never be broken.

"I'll adopt this boy!" she said. "He must have a special name, because he has been saved. Moses means 'drawn out of the water,' so that is what I shall call him. His name will be Moses."

Quickly she finished her bath, holding the child close as she left the river. Then a girl, whose name was Miriam, emerged from behind an olive tree.

"Would you like me to find a woman to nurse the child?" she asked.

Pharaoh's daughter smiled and nodded. Miriam ran toward town. Several minutes later, she came back with Moses' mother.

All became clear to us. The young girl was the boy's sister. The mother had put baby Moses into the basket, and Miriam had been watching all along to make sure her little brother wasn't harmed.

"Take this beautiful child," said Pharaoh's daughter, handing the baby to his mother. "Take good care of him and bring him back to live in the palace when he is about seven years old."

As Moses' mother held her son, the look on her face was like the warm sun. Shining with happiness and tears of joy, her face said it all. Her son was safe in her arms, and he had a future.

❧   ❧   ❧

Although Moses would learn important lessons in Pharaoh's court, he never forgot his own family. When he was grown, he saved the Hebrew people by leading them out of Egypt across the Red Sea toward a wonderful new land where they were free. Miriam was with him that day, shaking a tambourine, filled with joy because her people were finally saved from Pharaoh's brutal rule.

Yet that is another story for another day. You can see why we tell this one to our children first. Along with our bulrush friends, we were there at the beginning. So the next time a river brushes up against your feet or you hear us bullfrogs garumping, think of baby Moses and that long-ago day on the Nile River when we helped a little boy who would one day become a great leader.

᷍ ⚜ ᷍

From the Bible

The woman became pregnant and had a son. She saw there was something special about him and hid him. She hid him for three months. When she couldn't hide him any longer she got a little basket-boat made of papyrus, waterproofed it with tar and pitch, and placed the child in it. Then she set it afloat in the reeds at the edge of the Nile.

— Exodus 2:2-3

᷍ ⚜ ᷍

For Children

- How did Moses' mother draw on her faith when she put baby Moses in the basket? How can you tell?

- Why do you think Pharaoh's daughter rescued Moses?

- How do you see God working behind the scenes?

For Adults

Moses' mother found the strength and faith to set her son free, years ahead of when most sons and daughters naturally leave home. Had she not done so, the Israelites might not have escaped a life of brutal slavery in Egypt.

How have you set your children free? What has been the result? How has your faith helped you in that process? How might this story influence your relationship with your children? What are some of the joys of being a godparent or a grandparent?

May we, too, have the courage to send our children into the world, trusting God to light their way.

Chapter 4

Moses:
High on the Ten
Commandments

by Mount Sinai

I have been around for a long time. My name is Mount Sinai (pronounced sigh-nigh), and I am an enormous mountain. I came out of the deep nothingness when God's Spirit moved upon the earth's darkness at the very beginning of time.

You may think of mountains simply as cold, hard, dead, barren places of rock. Yet we flow with life from the deepest sources of the earth, where God first brought forth our boiling lava to make what you know as land. Deep, rumbling, molten earth flowed up through the waters, shooting high into the sky. Then everything settled back to rest, cool and quiet, ready for life to spring forth. Along with the waters, we are the ancestors of all. Solemn, sacred. Places of refuge and spirit.

We see very far from our great heights, and we have witnessed much. Like the fabric of our rock layers, we know that all life needs rules, clear guides on which to build straight paths. Let me tell you the story of God's rules, which the great Lord gave forth upon my shoulders to the man named Moses. I was there as a witness on that great day.

⌒⌒   ⌖   ⌒⌒

Moses had been walking across the desert for a long time, leading tens of thousands of Israelites (another name for the Hebrew people) through mountains and deserts, hills and valleys. He had freed the Israelites from slavery in Egypt, where they had been beaten mercilessly. Now he was taking them to their new home, many miles away.

"Moses, Moses, you will lead my people to a land flowing with milk and honey," God had told him. And Moses did, by following a pillar of fire by night, which rose up from my deep volcanic places, and a pillar of cloud by day.

The Israelites came closer and closer until they camped out, right beneath me. I could hear their voices, but they were not happy. They were grumbling and complaining.

"Moses, why did you bring us out here?"

"Moses, we miss the onions and leeks and fish and all the good things we had to eat back in Egypt!"

"We don't even know where we are going out here! At least when we were slaves, we had beds to sleep in and water to drink!"

The old man certainly had his hands full. Day after day, the people made him miserable, saying how much better life was back in Egypt. He called them stubborn and stiff-necked, and I guess they were. They fought with each other, and they fought with him. But they must have had good in them, because God was determined to bring them to a new land.

⌒⌒   ⌖   ⌒⌒

Moses liked to pray, and he often would ask God about where to lead the people. He would climb on my high shoulder ridges to talk with God, sometimes staying for weeks at a time. By walking right up to my cauldron and leaning in, he could feel the breath of God bubbling up from that deep ancient place. His face would shine, and everyone knew he had been in God's presence.

Then one day God told Moses to wash, to get the people ready, and to make them stand apart from me. They had to remain below on the flat plain while Moses climbed up to my highest heights. God was very clear about that. If they touched me, the great mountain, they would die. Throwing back his shoulders, Moses trod the familiar path up my side. Then God appeared, closer than ever before, unleashing his great power. Spewing out earthquakes and fire, I became ferocious for God, and for the people below. And the Lord thundered up from within me.

"I AM THE ONE who brought you out of Egypt."

"I AM your God, there is NO other!"

And then—quiet.

A quiet voice whispered on the wind for Moses' ear. And then he took tablets of my stone upon which to mark down God's rules as a gift for the people.

"No longer will these people be wanderers, but they will be my people, with a home," God said. "In following these rules, they will bless every land as a Promised Land."

God gave Moses ten rules.

God's people were not to steal or lie or yearn for things that were not theirs. They were to be faithful to their husbands and wives and to respect their parents. They were not to kill anyone or use God's name for bad purposes. They were not to

worship any idols—that is, someone who acted like God but wasn't. And they were to rest on Sunday, the sabbath, just like God rested when he finished creating the world.

God gave Moses and his people these rules out of love. Like any parent, he wanted them to be safe, to take care of themselves, and to treat others kindly.

The old man listened hard and chiseled the rules onto tablets of my stone. What the people did with them was another story.

At first, they resisted.

"Who needs rules?"

"We can make up gods of our own!"

God got so mad at the people that Moses had to plead for their very lives.

The people did move on, though, and learned the rules, which God called the commandments. And one day, the Israelites made it to a land where many of their descendants live to this very day.

We mountains are old and have long, long memories. We have seen much and know much and trust much. Every so often when I rumble and throw off a little smoke, I remember those days, those moments between God and Moses on my highest heights, those miraculous days when God's people were given the ten rules for building lives.

✿　✿　✿

From the Bible

Mount Sinai was all smoke because GOD had come down on it as fire. Smoke poured from it like smoke from a furnace. The whole mountain shuddered in huge spasms.

—EXODUS 19:18

The Ten Commandments

God said,

> *Do not worship any other gods but me.*
> *Do not worship any likeness of me.*
> *Do not misuse my name.*
> *Remember to keep the sabbath holy.*
> *Honor your father and your mother.*
> *You shall not kill.*
> *You shall not commit adultery.*
> *You shall not steal.*
> *You shall not testify falsely against your neighbor.*
> *You shall not covet anything that is your neighbor's.*

— ADAPTED FROM
EXODUS 20:1-17

For Children

• Why do you think God gives us rules?

• What does it mean to "honor your father and your mother"?

• Why does God care about how we act?

For Adults

Parents set rules for their children to help them be safe and to help them grow into the best people they can be. God does the same thing by setting boundaries and rules for all of us. As your children grow older, show them that your decisions are not unilateral, but that you are following God's moral compass points.

Are there any commandments that you have trouble keeping? How might you ask God to help you? How might you better stay away from temptations? How can you show God's loving presence when your child disappoints you and breaks the rules? How might you talk about God's authority in your life?

God eventually provided Moses with seventy helpers to aid him in leading God's people through the wilderness. Through this process, Moses learned that receiving help along the journey is a holy and blessed endeavor. In the wild areas of your life, how might you best find and use help from other people?

Chapter 5

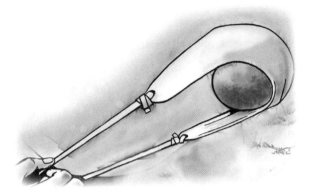

David: A Rock in the Right Place

by the Slingshot

I am a slingshot, a small and humble weapon that can launch rocks through the air. Long ago, I protected a shepherd boy named David in the hills outside Bethlehem. He used me to defend against the lions and bears that tried to eat his sheep. One day, though, I fought something much more fearsome and powerful than a wild animal. I was used in a battle against a giant, a real live giant, who threatened the very survival of God's people.

The day started out well enough. David, the youngest of seven sons, was called in from the fields by his father, Jesse, to take food to three of his brothers. They were soldiers, off fighting the Philistines.

David was loaded down with cheese, bread, dried fish, and figs, but there was still room for me in his pocket. I figured it would be an easy trip. Little did I know what awaited us.

"Bring me back some news," said his father. "I want to know my sons are alive!"

In those days there were no phones or mailboxes or computers, so parents had no way to hear from their children when they were away. Like all parents, Jesse wanted to know that his boys were safe and would be home soon.

✑ ✑ ✑

Trouble awaited us at the front line of the battle. David's brothers, and all the men of the Israelite army, had been taunted for forty days straight by a giant called Goliath. They were in no mood to report news to their little brother.

"Get outta here, kid," said one.

"Go back home and play with your toys," said another.

"This isn't a game," muttered the third.

Goliath reminded me of a volcano, with steam and thunder coming out of the top. He was almost as tall as a house and made everyone around him look tiny. He was covered in armor so he clanked when he walked, and he carried a sword that looked as though it could slice a tree in half.

"Send just one soldier out," he demanded. "One man. I will fight him. If he wins, we will become your slaves. If he loses—and I know he will—you and your families will serve us. Forever!"

David knew that his people had been slaves long ago. They had earned their freedom after great hardship and would rather die than lose it again.

But Goliath was a terrifying force, and he jeered at everyone he saw. "Is there no one willing to stand up to me? Are you all COWARDS?"

Soon David grew angry. "Who does that man think he is? He is making fun of God's army!"

꘠ ꕔ ꘠

Every morning Goliath came out of his camp and dared the Israelites to fight. Every morning—and evening and afternoon—there was no one brave enough to face him. The Israelites began to wonder what it would be like to lose the war.

One morning Goliath was particularly irritating. "Go home and get your dogs," he jeered. "Bring them back! Maybe they could fight better than you wimps! At least they would snarl!"

David suddenly reached for me, his slingshot, as he did when we went after lions or bears. I knew what he wanted—to stand up and fight, to protect his people.

Next thing I knew, we were standing in front of King Saul, asking for permission to fight the giant!

"I will kill Goliath with my slingshot," David said, holding me up. "Let me at him."

The great king sighed. "Kid, go home. I'm busy running a war."

David drew his shoulders back and gripped me tightly. I knew he trusted me—but more important, he trusted God.

"I've killed lions and bears," he said. "God has always protected me. He will protect me now, and we WILL win."

Saul paused, thinking. For a moment he seemed to take David seriously. But he also knew a wrong decision would cost the boy his life. And the Israelites their freedom.

The king took a deep breath.

"The Lord will keep me safe," David repeated, squeezing me tightly.

"What do I have to lose?" said Saul. "Wear this armor, and go in the name of the One who created you!"

✑ ✦ ✑

Finally David had the king's blessing to fight Goliath. Wearing the breastplate, helmet, and sword provided by King Saul, we clanked away, weighed down by metal but light in spirit.

A half mile away, David threw off the heavy armor, leaving it in the dust. Kneeling by the first stream we came across, he picked up five smooth stones and loaded me with the first.

Together we strode toward the hill where the giant held forth. Insults flew from both armies, yet David stood tall and firm in his resolve. After spending many nights alone with only the sheep and stars for friends, David knew how to summon courage.

Suddenly, a bone-chilling taunt thundered across the battlefield.

"Is this the best your king can do? You are just a silly boy!" Goliath jeered, leaping in front of us. "Children belong at home with their mothers!"

The soldiers gasped.

Goliath's face was red, his skin rough. He spit and swore. Sunlight glanced off his sharp spear as if it were a lightning bolt.

"You come to me with weapons," David said. "I come to you in the name of the living God!"

"You're nothing but a miserable flea!" roared Goliath. "Go home!"

"Everyone here knows that God will deliver you into our hands," said David.

Froth dripped from the giant's mouth.

"God, you are my sword and shield," said David. "Use me as you will!"

Goliath could take no more and narrowed his eyes. Like a cat toying with a mouse, he lunged for us, ready to do his worst.

In that half second, David held me up and aimed me dead center between Goliath's eyes. We launched a first rock, then a second, then a third.

Still the giant stomped forward, hurling his huge body toward us like a boulder.

"Remember the lions," David whispered.

I knew what he meant. We had killed several lions out in the fields when they threatened the sheep. Sometimes it took more than a few rocks to bring them down.

Then, just as Goliath's outstretched arm reached for us, he thudded to the earth, shaking the ground for miles. His spear cracked, his sword broke under the weight of his body, and his horrible voice was never heard again.

✎ ✎ ✎

Like bats flying out of a cave, the Philistines turned and fled in all directions. Cheering and holding their swords high, some of the Israelites chased after them. Others surrounded David, trying to lift him over their heads in celebration.

Never again did his brothers say David was too little to be of use. He was more than their equal, for he grew to be a mighty king, the greatest king in all of Israel.

My working days as a weapon are over now. Yet every so often, David will take me out of his pocket and hold me for a moment, remembering that day.

I know what he is doing. He's saying a prayer, thanking God. David is a real king, and real kings know they never fight on their own. A real king is big enough to know that God always stands by his side.

✐ ✦ ✐

From the Bible

David answered, "You come at me with sword and spear and battle-ax. I come at you in the name of GOD-of-the-Angel-Armies, the God of Israel's troops, whom you curse and mock. This very day GOD is handing you over to me. I'm about to kill you, cut off your head, and serve up your body and the bodies of your Philistine buddies to the crows and coyotes. The whole earth will know that there's an extraordinary God in Israel."

— 1 SAMUEL 17:45-46

✐ ✦ ✐

For Children

- David was brave and helped God. How do you help God?

- Do you ever feel that people think you are too young to do important things? Can you think of an example?

- David asked God for help to get him through a battle with the Philistines. When do you ask God for help? What happens when you do?

For Adults

We may think that children are too small to advance God's work in the world, but God often chooses the youngest or most marginalized among us to do great works. How might you honor that model with the young people in your life? How might you most effectively model a life of Christian commitment that says God stands by your side?

Do your children, grandchildren, or other children in your care ever see you pray? Teach them through your example, praying both spontaneously and at designated times, such as grace before meals and prayers before school or bedtime. They will surprise you with what they learn—and share!

Chapter 6

Deborah: Charging for God

by the Stallion

If I were in a restaurant, I'd squeeze into a chair, put my front hooves on the table, and order grass for dinner. And grass for dessert. And maybe a little side salad of grass. Forget all that stiff hay that other horses eat. Too crunchy.

And forget the restaurant, anyway. I'm a free-range kind of horse, a big black Arabian stallion with a love for—you guessed it—grass. Whenever I see even a patch of it, I'll gallop over and start the Great Stallion Roll. I'm on my back, with my legs kicking in the air, my whole body covered with that fresh grassy smell.

There's one thing that will make me leave the field. Deborah, my lovely, brave owner. When she whistles, I scramble up and streak to her side. I still remember the day when she took me into battle. I was at the front leading the

41

charge, followed by thousands of soldiers. Deborah rode me in the spirit of a warrior, confident and in charge.

❧ ❧ ❧

Deborah didn't plan to be a warrior. At first she was happy being a judge, which was a rare position for a woman in those days. Her court was a bare hillside under a palm tree. Wise and steady, she helped people solve their problems before things got out of control. That's why she worried about the trouble happening over the hills.

Our enemies, the Canaanites, (pronounced K-na-nights) had been invading nearby towns for years. They would take people captive and carry them off to strange lands. Our townspeople tried to ignore the threat, thinking it would never happen to them. But they were kidding themselves. Deborah knew there was danger so she decided to call on General Barak, the head of our army.

❧ ❧ ❧

"We can't wait much longer," she said. "The Canaanites will try to capture us one day soon. You must do something. You must take our army and fight. Defeat them for good, so we can sleep in peace."

"Chariots," Barak said. "Deborah, they have chariots and swords and spears. They're much better equipped than we are. They'll make horse meat out of us."

Horse meat? Horse meat!! *Hmmmmph,* I snorted loudly. Horse meat was not a pleasant thought.

"You must go," she said. "We cannot wait any longer."

Barak looked her straight in the eye.

"Then you go with me," he said. "That is the only way I will fight."

Neeeigghhhhh!!! My stallion pulse pounded.

Women weren't on the battlefields in those days. They stayed back, taking care of children and running their homes. Yet I knew there was no one braver than Deborah.

She looked toward her house. A small hand waved. It was her daughter.

"I'll do it," she said. "To keep them safe. To keep all of us safe."

Then she whistled for me, her steed.

Together. We would do it together!

☙　☙　☙

That very night, ten thousand men and one woman, Deborah, gathered under the cover of darkness. Preparing themselves for battle, they knelt in prayer. "We are your people, Lord. Guard us, protect us, and deliver us from harm's way."

Shivers ran through me as I took my place at the head of the line. It was a stallion's dream.

Mile by mile, we moved quietly through the darkness. Before dawn we were on top of Mount Tabor, looking down at the flat, fertile plain below. But word had leaked out that we were on our way, for the enemy was amassed there, ready to fight.

"C'mon down! You're no match for us!" shouted Sisera, the Canaanite general. We had heard about him. He was a cruel man, a man of no mercy.

"Did you miss your sleep last night? You're probably too weak to fight us," taunted another.

"Yeah, just surrender. Less pain that way..."

Thousands of Canaanite soldiers, protected with heavy armor, stretched for miles on the plain, just across the river. Handsome horses pulled heavy iron chariots with wheels flashing like they were on fire.

Barak shook his head.

"Watch out for those chariots," he said. "They have about nine hundred of them. Don't jump up on them, even if you get close, because sharp knives are tied onto each wheel. They're flashing now because they're reflecting the sun's rays."

Neeeighhhhhh!!! Knives tied to chariot wheels, right at the level of our chests? Yikes! *Neeeighhhhhh!!!*

Shudders ran through the men. And me.

"Do not fear," said Deborah. "God will protect us. Remember our ancestors! God parted the Red Sea so they could be free. He split rocks in the desert so they could have water. He made bread fall from the skies so they would not starve. He will protect us just the same."

⌒ ⌘ ⌒

And then we waited. We waited for Deborah to hear from God that it was time to fight. One day turned into another as the Canaanites taunted us from below.

"Hey, scaredy-cats! Come out and play with the big kids!"

Why didn't they come up after us? There were rugged paths up the hill, even a dusty road. They could cross that river on the plain and be right at our throats. They could move off that grass. Grass! Tasty grass. Body-rubbing grass, soft and fragrant. They could move off that grass, and it would be all mine.

Then, one morning as I was lost in such daydreams, Deborah looked to the sky, turned to Barak and said: "NOW! God says the time is now!"

With his hand raised to signal the troops, Barak bound forward and we raced into formation.

◦◦◦ ◦◦◦ ◦◦◦

It had rained all night, a gentle pounding that left the ground refreshed. As we thundered down the hill, the wind was at our backs and pushed us even faster. Horses can gallop through anything, and our foot soldiers raced nimbly behind us. Nothing would stop us. We had people at home to protect.

Minute by minute, the rains grew heavier, blowing straight ahead. Thunder and lightening boomed and flashed, along with one particularly eerie sound: the clicking of the knives on Canaanite chariot wheels.

Boom! Flash! Click! Flash! Click! We could see the river rising and the ground getting muddy, as the Canaanites marched forward, their hate-filled faces coming into focus.

And then it happened. Just as we prepared to swim and lunge through the river, torrents of water spilled over the riverbanks, swamping the ground below. Those lovely grass fields were suddenly mud pools, leaving all nine hundred chariots stuck in the muck. No longer did their wheels roll. No longer did their knives clack.

Now I knew why the Canaanites hadn't surged the hill. Their chariots only worked on dry and flat ground.

"This was God's work," said Deborah. "No wonder we had to wait. God made it rain so that the river would rise!"

For the Canaanites, the battle was over. They raised their hands in defeat. Except for one figure off to the side, limping into the woods. Sisera, the leader of the Canaanite army, was trying to escape. Deborah watched him, gave a small smile, and encouraged Barak to turn the troops homeward. *Odd,* I thought. *Odd.* Why not go after him? Why was she letting such an evil man slip away?

⌒ ⧉ ⌒

Deborah has returned to her role as a judge and a wife and a mother. I live happily in my field, enjoying all the grass I could ever want. All of our soldiers have returned to their families, and everyone is now safely out of danger, thanks to the soldiers' bravery. Peace—and God—again rule our land.

And Sisera, that mean general? Turns out that he stumbled into the home of a woman named Jael. She quietly punished him for his evil deeds so that he would never hurt anyone again.

⌒ ⧉ ⌒

From the Bible

Then you, Deborah, rose up; you got up, a mother in Israel. God chose new leaders, who then fought at the gates.

— JUDGES 5:7B-8A

⌒ ⧉ ⌒

For Children

• Describe a time in which you were courageous for God.

• What does it mean to wait for "God's time"?

• Why did the soldiers pray before the battle?

• What might you say to God if you are scared?

For Adults

No doubt Deborah and Barak would have preferred to stay at home, but like many of us, they protected and served their community and those they loved. They acted with courage, and they also depended on God.

Name a time when you have found a strong balance between action and faith. In what ways does your profession or vocation allow you to serve others? How do you draw on God for strength? Deborah had vision and courage. Barak listened to her and was able to use her skills in his work. Are there ways in which you might better incorporate the gifts of those around you toward God's end?

Chapter 7

Daniel:
Not So Good a Snack

by the Lion

Abig lion like me appreciates the finer things in life, like the sun, good food, and toys to bat around. If you have a cat at home, you might just think of me as a big cat. I like the same things, except I'll eat anything that is thrown to me.

If someone happens to drop in, so to speak, I'll have him—or her—for lunch. "Drop in any time," I say. Like over the fence.

I used to work for the king, and he kept me fierce and hungry. When he wanted to punish someone, he tossed him into my den and my friends and I would eat him up. A horrible custom, I must admit...although I didn't exactly mind munching up bad guys. It was my civic duty.

The story I'm going to tell you happened a long, long time ago. No one throws people to us anymore, and even I'm kind of glad about that.

✑ ⚜ ✑

I watched this fellow on the other side of the fence before I came nose-to-nose with him. His name was Daniel, and he was a good man. He was honest and bright and true and kind, and King Darius had put him in charge of one hundred and twenty princes.

Every morning Daniel would walk by my cage on the way to his job at the palace. Then, three times a day, he would leave and walk back home. I heard that he was going back to his home to pray by the side of his bed. There, he would kneel, tell God everything, listen for advice, and then go back to work, grounded in faith.

He didn't stop to look at me much, or to admire how muscular and scary I am. Sometimes, though, he'd glance at me out of the corner of his eye, and I'd growl in return. We lions are pretty tough, you know. I'm sure I scared him, so I don't know why he often smiled after he saw me.

✑ ⚜ ✑

One day a bad wind blew through the kingdom. It was days since we'd eaten, and all the lions were famished. My stomach was growling, wondering what—or who—would be our next meal. I'd have gone for dandelions at that point, but I did hope for something meatier, something more filling.

Suddenly two men walked by, their heads bent low. Their eyes shifted like my tail does when I smell lunch. And I could feel it twitching.

"King Darius is going to put Daniel in charge of the whole kingdom," whispered one. "He says he's such a fine leader that he will now rule over all of us!"

Enraged, his friend grew red-faced. "Unthinkable!" he said. "We don't need Daniel! We don't want anyone telling us what to do!"

His friend agreed, waving his arms angrily. *Hmmm,* I thought. *That man looks tasty.*

"We'll show the king that Daniel is only out for himself! We'll get rid of him!"

Just out of earshot of my cage, they stopped, gestured wildly, and pointed to Daniel's bedroom window. Then they headed toward the palace. I knew one thing for certain. They were up to no good.

❧ ❦ ❧

A few days later the gate was finally opened, and a man was tossed into our cage. Famished, I raced for him, eager to gulp him down quickly so I wouldn't have to share.

Opening my jaws wide, I lunged. But then I froze.

The man they had thrown to us was Daniel!

He turned and looked me straight in the eye. Saying nothing, he dropped to his knees.

This is new, I thought. Someone sees how all-powerful I am! Kneeling before me is good.

Then I realized he was praying to God.

"I put myself in your hands, Lord," he said. "I entrust my life to you."

Hungry as I was, I clamped my mouth shut. My powerful paws did not flatten him. I couldn't eat this man, for he had God's hand upon him. I knew it. I felt it. So I let him live.

There are some things worth going hungry for, and this was one of them. Daniel and I and the other lions spent the night under the stars together. We let him rest with us as a friend. He was safe.

ⅇ𝒻ᴼ ᵕᵕ ⅇ𝒻ᴼ

When the sun rose, I could hear crying from the other side of the gate. It turned out to be King Darius, worried sick over the loss of such a good man. He had been unable to sleep all night.

Daniel, whole and sound, stood tall in our cage without a scratch. The king saw him and was filled with joy. Immediately he gave orders to open the gate and release him.

I later found out why Daniel was thrown into my cage. The men walking by that day were jealous of Daniel because he trusted God, not the king, to lead him. Knowing that Daniel prayed to God three times a day for help, they wrote out a new law and tricked the king into signing it. If anyone asked God for help and guidance instead of the king, the law said, he would be thrown to the lions. Even though Daniel knew about the new law, he continued doing what he believed was right—he kept praying to God every day. He would kneel and ask for God's help in everything.

One more matter. You know those men who tried to get rid of Daniel? The ones who arranged to have him thrown to us?

Well, let's just say they never bothered anyone again. I'm proud to say I had a hand, or should I say a paw, in that accomplishment. They were quite tasty.

From the Bible
When Daniel learned that the decree had been signed and posted, he continued to pray just as he had always done. His house had windows in the upstairs that opened toward Jerusalem. Three times a day he knelt there in prayer, thanking and praising his God.

— DANIEL 6:10

For Children:

- Talking to God—silently or aloud—is called prayer, and God always wants to hear from us. Daniel knelt by his bed and prayed three times a day when he wanted to thank God or needed God's help. When do you pray? What do you pray for?

- What kinds of things might you thank God for? What kinds of things might you ask for? What kinds of things might you say "I'm sorry" for?

- Why is it important to talk to God when you are happy as well as when you are sad?

For Adults

Although it is important to pray with our children, our own prayer lives become shallow if we don't have our own time with God. Because of his grounded prayer life, Daniel had the strength to face bad-tempered rulers and hungry lions. He also set an example for those around him.

What steps might you take to deepen your prayer life? Daniel worked for the king, yet still sought divine guidance for matters large and small. How might you bring faith to your work life? If you are new to prayer, try this: thank God for your blessings every day, especially specific ones. Ask for forgiveness, pray for others, and request visible signs of God's presence in your life that day. Let people know you are praying for them. If someone is troubled, try offering a prayer on the spot, if appropriate.

Chapter 8

Gabrielle and the Great Message

by the Novice Angel

I'm a novice Archangel (pronounced ark-angel), a very new angel learning the ropes in heaven. Gabrielle is my teacher up here, and she shows me all the ways that we work for God to help humanity.

Even though Gabrielle is wrinkled with age, her face is bright and lively, much like the colors she twists around herself for clothes. From the sunset she'll grab a bit of orange. Blue comes from the ocean, yellow from daffodils. For scarlet, she flies down into volcanoes and pulls out red-hot lava, stretching it out until it cools. Twisting those colors around herself for a dress, she'll then arrange her wispy gray hair into sparkly webs around her head.

Tall, slender, and calm, she moves so fast and gracefully that she reminds me of a gazelle. Maybe that is why God chose her for one of his most important tasks.

⌒∕ ⌒⌖⌒ ⌒∕

That special morning all of us clustered around God's heavenly throne. As angels, we all have our regular jobs: six-winged Cherubim angels praise God and guard the throne. Dominion angels help God look after whole countries. Fiery Virtue angels care for the stars and planets. And Archangels, like Gabrielle, deliver messages and fight cosmic battles.

"Gabrielle!" came God's voice that morning, deep and mellow, loving and kind.

"Yes, Lord?"

"Gabrielle, this day I have a special task for you. One that will, I hope, change the world. Today I entrust to you my message for a young woman, a girl named Mary. In her world she is but a teenager, one whose heart and voice is often overlooked.

"This day she is to have the choice of a lifetime. I want her to be a bridge between heaven and earth."

I was excited by the news. Mary would be offered the most sacred gift, entrusted to only a few—to be a bridge!

"You will find her at home in the town of Nazareth."

Wow! This was big! I looked at Gabrielle and could feel my heart thump.

It was the only sound in the room. Here in heaven, where you can always hear the sounds of music and the *whrrrrr* of creation, all activity stopped. Cherubim jerked back the wings from their faces and stared wide-eyed. Several moons careened wildly across the sky as the Virtues lost track of wayward planets.

Then, *whumpf!* Gabrielle's great wings unfurled, ready for flight.

"Nothing," she had once told me, "must stop or slow down a request from God."

"Lord, what is it that you would have me say to Mary?" she asked.

"For the sake of the world, I want her to be the mother of my Son, Jesus. Tell her that it is I, the Lord, who asks this."

WHAT? I thought. *A young girl would bear the son of God? A teenager would be his mother?*

If the old angel was in shock, she didn't show it. A slight flick of her wrist told me that I was to join her, and I went to her side. Silent and invisible, I too would visit Mary. I was thrilled.

∞ ⋄ ∞

When we arrived, Mary was alone, sweeping out one of two rooms where she lived with her family. Hers was a small, simple home, like the others bordering it. She gasped when she looked up to see Gabrielle's magnificent form filling the doorway. The tall, willowy angel moved toward her, wings brushing the ceiling, colors shimmering. Mary clutched her broom for protection, since Gabrielle must have looked like a truly strange being to her.

Quietly invisible, I watched and listened. I liked this girl already.

"Mary, you are favored in God's eyes. The Lord is with you," Gabrielle said.

Still holding the broomstick, Mary backed against the wall, a stool clattering to the floor behind her.

Mary knew that God's favor could be dangerous in her troubled land where a Roman king, Herod, ruled and often punished her people. Yet the girl's raised eyebrows and open mouth beckoned Gabrielle to say more.

"Mary, you will conceive and bear a son, and his name will be Jesus. He will be called the Son of the Most High, God's Son, and of his kingdom there will be no end."

Her response was almost a whisper.

"How can this be?"

I understood. She was engaged to Joseph, a carpenter, but they were not yet married. Her first thought was of him, to whom she had promised the rest of her life.

"Do not be afraid," said Gabrielle. "The power of the Most High will overshadow you."

As if a great weight had fallen on her, Mary's knees began to buckle.

Gabrielle reached out, surrounding and supporting her with her glorious wings.

"Do not fear, dear. Do not be afraid. The Lord is with you, and I am as well."

Mary took several deep breaths, then looked up into the angel's warm eyes and smiled.

She will be fine, I thought. *It will be all right.*

"Let it be with me," she said softly, "according to your word."

Hallelujah! The message had been delivered.

And Jesus would have a good mother, I could tell. Someone who would ponder things, who would do her best, someone who would take things moment by moment, in God's time. Someone who would hug Jesus when he was scared, someone who would teach him that all would be well.

Ꙩ ꙩ Ꙩ

As Gabrielle floated out the door, there was a tremendous rustling above, so loud that it caught me off guard. I glanced back at Mary. Would she be startled? But she was busy sweeping, finishing her chores.

She had put her trust in God, and her heart was calm. She could not hear the noise above in heaven, but I knew those sounds. Thousands and thousands of angels were beating their wings, creating a drumbeat of alleluias rolling through heaven and earth.

And that beating, that great rustling, is still there. The angels are still overjoyed about Jesus' birth.

And by watching Gabrielle, I learned how to deliver God's messages kindly and with care.

We still give thanks every time a person says "Yes" to what God asks of them. So listen carefully. Listen for the angels, for the music of heaven, and for God's voice. You never know what a day might bring.

Ꙩ ꙩ Ꙩ

From the Bible

And Mary said, I'm bursting with God-news; I'm dancing the song of my Savior God. God took one good look at me, and look what happened—I'm the most fortunate woman on earth! What God has done for me will never be forgotten, the God whose very name is holy, set apart from all others.

— LUKE 1:46-49

~ ~ ~

For Children

Mary was just a teenager when Gabrielle asked her to bear God's son, Jesus. She could have said no, but said yes, even though she was scared.

- Have you asked for God's help when you were scared? What was the result?

- What do you think God might be asking you to do?

- The angel Gabrielle brought Mary the good news about Jesus. Have you ever seen, or experienced in some way, an angel? What messages do you think angels might bring?

For Adults

Visualize yourself standing next to Mary as she hears the angel's request; next to Joseph as he hears his fiancée is pregnant and decides to leave her; next to the shepherds in the fields, hearing a chorus of angels singing. And then remember Mary's response: "Let it be with me according to your word." To what extent would it make a difference in your life if you met the Christmas story head-on, aside from the cultural and economic frenzy that happens in December?

What might Mary's reaction to God's unexpected plan mean for your life? It is easy to take Jesus, Mary, and Joseph for granted. What if Mary had said no? Would Jesus have been born? God has great faith in children and teenagers. How might that shape your relationships with them? How might that change your expectations?

Chapter 9

Blazing a Path for Jesus

by the Star of Bethlehem

I am a star, a white-hot star. From my place in the heavens I have burned for millions of years. One eon can seem very much like another in the depths and loneliness of space. Yet when God flung us—stars, planets, and moons—into the heavens, he gave us a job no one else has.

"Without you, my people would look up and see nothing but blackness," God said. "And my world is never black. I want my people to know that even in the darkest nights, I am there. You will remind them of that."

Burning as points of light across the sky, we were delighted when people learned to chart their travels by us. In ships at sea, they would count on us to point them toward safe harbors. In the deserts, we would be their only source of light.

Sometimes we would watch couples in love, dancing the night away under our glittering sparkles.

The centuries passed like this, without much change, until one very special night.

From the warm blue planet Earth, we heard a cry that sang to the universe—the cry of a newborn child, pulling us in like a magnet. We searched out the source immediately.

It was Jesus, born as a human baby! New, and full of young life, he was snuggled into a young woman's arms. Hungry and then sleepy, like any other baby, he needed comfort and warm blankets and milk.

A simple carpenter, Joseph, was there to guard him as his earthly father, and the young girl Mary was his mother. They were sleeping in a stable, of all places, bedding down with the animals. Jesus' first bed was a manger, the big wooden trough that animals ate from.

All creation said hello and embraced him. The strong wood of that manger protected him. The wool threads of the blanket kept him warm. Cawing and baaing and snorting, birds and lambs and goats surrounded him, each singing their own special lullaby. But there was a problem. They were in the dark. Using the light from only one oil lamp, Mary and Joseph could barely see Jesus. And Jesus couldn't see the animals at all.

This was my moment. No. This was *Jesus'* moment.

I wanted Jesus to know he had come to a magnificent, happy place: Earth. I wanted Mary and Joseph to see how beautiful their little boy was. I wanted Jesus to be able to see the donkey that had nudged his way into the stable, the lambs that had not eaten because the manger was full of baby instead of hay, and the Bethlehem mice that were running toward his little bed.

Entire armies of angels sang the most beautiful music. Heaven and earth united in joy, rid forever of our loneliness. As I laid a shimmering bright path of light toward Jesus, the stable glowed as if it were daylight. And then I softened my beam a bit, for babies have a lot of work to do, just being babies. Jesus would change the world, but he needed to sleep first.

↔

The angels couldn't keep the good news to themselves, and why should they? Dancing, flying, and singing, they approached shepherds in the fields near Bethlehem, singing: "Glory to God in the highest heaven, and peace on earth to all whom God loves!"

Stunned, the shepherds grabbed for their sheep. Who were these wild creatures?

"Do not be afraid," said an angel. "The Lord, the King of Peace, the Son of God, is born this night in the city of Bethlehem. Go and see!"

I raised my fire and lighted every inch of their path, making sure the shepherds did not stumble. This was the most important journey of their lives, and I would make the way clear. Shepherds lay down their lives to protect their sheep, and those brave men and boys would want to see the holy one who would, one day, be known as the Good Shepherd.

↔

I knew there would be more visitors to follow. Sure enough, travelers from the East appeared: three wise men, carrying gifts for the newborn King. Staying ablaze for weeks, I lighted the way until they, too, could kneel before Jesus and offer their gifts of gold and frankincense and myrrh.

But my starlight work was not done.

᧨ ᧨ ᧨

One night not long after Jesus was born, Joseph awoke suddenly. He told Mary that an angel had warned him in a dream to take her and Jesus and run. Their lives were in danger. Herod, the Roman ruler, was threatened by the attention the little one was getting. He was on the hunt to find the child and kill him, if he could.

The Holy Family left that very night for Egypt. I knew they had to stay hidden, so I dimmed my glow, leaving just enough light to guide their footsteps. When they couldn't get Jesus to sleep, I would send a comforting ray of light to him. When Joseph went in search of food, I would light his path. And when Mary, who pondered everything in her heart, grew a little scared, I would burn more brightly. The Holy Family reached Egypt safely. I had performed my task with happiness and love, lighting the way for my dear Lord.

That is a star's best job after all: to find Jesus and to help others see him.

I am told that he will come to earth again someday. I only hope he comes at night, so that I may blaze the heavens for him one more time.

᧨ ᧨ ᧨

From the Bible

Instructed by the king, they set off. Then the star appeared again, the same star they had seen in the eastern skies. It led them on until it hovered over the place of the child. They could hardly contain themselves. They were in the right place! They had arrived at the right time!

—MATTHEW 2:9-10

◌ ◌◌ ◌

For Children

- When Jesus was born, there were no cell phones, no TVs, no computers. Yet God put the word out about Jesus' birth through the Star of Bethlehem and mighty angels. What would it have been like to be in Bethlehem that night?

- God used light from the star to direct Mary and Joseph to safety. God leads us from darkness into light. What does that mean?

- Memorize this line: "The light shines in the darkness, and the darkness has not overcome it." Jesus is the light. Follow the light.

For Adults

The Star of Bethlehem lit the way to Jesus' birthplace so that the three wise men might find the Son of God and worship him. This story, and the visualization of the star's experiences, is written to encourage young ones to learn that even creation serves God. To what extent does the natural world help you find God? Where and how does that best happen? How might you share that experience with your children or grandchildren?

Like the Star of Bethlehem, we too are called to help others know the life of Christ, especially in dark moments. Is that hard for you? While good works are essential in the Christian life, so is talking about God. When and how have you been successful in lighting the path for others on their spiritual journey? How might you do so in the future?

Chapter 10

Food for Me, Food for All

by the Ant

I had my eye on the boy, but mostly on the lunch basket he carried with him. Ah, lunch. Through the Ant News Station, I'd heard he was toting smoked fish and home-made barley bread, still warm from his mother's oven. Don't ask to see the Ant News. For you, it would be like looking at a screen the size of a pea. You'll just have to trust me to tell you the truth.

I did get some lunch—but more important, on that day, the day of the Great Miracle, I saw Jesus! Given my affection for food, it was one of the best days of my life. Jesus fed over five thousand people…and me.

Here's how it happened. I was enjoying a dead cockroach for breakfast, when a terribly large object crashed down on me. Everything was dark, but it suddenly smelled delicious. I had been covered by the basket of bread!

The boy had set it right down on top of me, and thank goodness I was still alive. Warm bread wins over dead bugs any day, so I squeezed upward through the crisscrossed wicker with visions of sweet barley filling my tiny ant head.

Ah, but his mother had wrapped all five loaves in palm branches. Tight as a drum and impossible to chew through. Then, voices. Suddenly I heard loud, excited voices.

"You can't believe what he can do!"

"He healed my sister. She's been sick for years and she's fine now!"

"My father was blind and now he can see!"

"He raised a girl from the dead!"

Hmmm…what was going on? I'd never heard such a ruckus.

Bam! Bam! Suddenly, the basket flew up as the boy grabbed it, swinging me around as he ran.

Then came more voices, yelling, all around us.

"It's Jesus!"

"It's him!"

"Wow, he's tall…"

"Jesus, heal me! I want to walk more than anything!"

Bump. Scrape. Ooomp. We were getting pretty jostled by the crowd. *Up. Down. Up. Sideways. Down.* I held on tight to the basket's side. Sometimes the boy would even carry it on his head to squeeze through the crowd.

Crawling to the top, I peeked out at the crowd. I saw a crippled woman, carried on a blanket by two small boys who looked just like her. Heaving and lurching, they brought her to the man who was causing all the excitement. There he was, Jesus!

I watched, fascinated, my antennae waving with curiosity. As he knelt beside her, everyone else grew quiet. All of Jesus' attention was focused on her. With one hand resting over his heart and the other touching her cheek, Jesus looked into her eyes and said just six words: "Be healed. Rise up and walk!"

She shuddered. And then her cheeks became rosy again as she stood up and reached for her boys, gathering them close.

"Thank you, oh, thank you," she said, through her tears of joy.

"We can never do enough for you," said one boy.

"You have given us our mother back!" said the other.

And so it went. Jesus laid his hands on people, and they were instantly healed. The blind could see. The deaf could hear. Sad and troubled people began to smile. Finally, as evening approached, the sun began to drop in the sky.

♋ ♣ ♋

"Jesus, it's getting late, and these people are hungry," said one of his friends. "Tell them to go buy food for themselves."

"Philip, you give them something to eat," came the reply.

"But we have no food!" stammered Philip, "not enough for all these people...."

"Then find some," came Jesus' reply.

By this time, the boy had grown tired. Drowsing off with his head on the basket, he was suddenly nudged awake by the man who had been talking to Jesus.

"Boy! Do you have food with you?"

Wearily the child nodded.

"Five loaves and two fish inside my basket..."

"We need them," said the man. "Jesus needs them."

✑ ✦ ✑

I can't tell you how it happened, because I still don't know for sure. Philip handed the fish and bread over, and Jesus put his hands on them. Then I blinked. In that instant, there was suddenly enough food for everybody, mountains of loaves and fishes! Thousands of people ate and ate.

No one was left hungry. Everyone was full, saying it was the best food they'd ever had.

"Bring me whatever is left," said Jesus. "Find all the broken pieces and bring them to me."

Twelve baskets of leftovers were handed to him. One by one, Jesus touched them. Then, picking up the boy's basket, on which I still clung, he said, "Thank you, God. Thank you for all you give us. Thank you for those who share. Thank you for each other."

Putting the basket down, Jesus carefully held out his little finger toward me. I crawled onto it, looking straight into his face. As he gave me a ride to the ground on his hand, he leaned over and whispered, "Hi, little one. I knew you were there all the time. Did you get enough to eat?"

I nodded, my antennae bobbing up and down like springs.

"Good," he said. "I'll always take care of you. Don't forget."

And I haven't. When Jesus shows up, there's more than enough food—and love—to go around.

From the Bible

"There's a little boy here who has five barley loaves and two fish. But that's a drop in the bucket for a crowd like this." Jesus said, "Make the people sit down." There was a nice carpet of green grass in this place. They sat down, about five thousand of them. Then Jesus took the bread and, having given thanks, gave it to those who were seated. He did the same with the fish. All ate as much as they wanted.

— John 6:9-11

For Children

- Jesus paid attention to the needs of others. Have you ever noticed when someone needed something and you helped them? Tell the story.

- What might it have been like to see Jesus doing miracles? Is there a miracle you would hope for?

- Jesus fed thousands of people with very little food. How do you think he multiplied all those loaves and fishes?

- Have you ever felt what it is like to not have enough food to eat? Have you ever been homeless? What was that like?

- By sharing, the boy was able to help feed others. What might you share to help others?

For Adults

The boy was responsible about keeping his basket safe from harm. He was a good steward. In what ways are you a good steward of those things God has entrusted to you? When the time came, the boy was willing to share what he had. He took a small step forward, and Jesus did the rest. Are there ways in which you might take a small step toward caring for others, even if you have little yourself?

Who taught you about giving, and what difference has it made? How might you model this type of stewardship in your life? Have you ever witnessed a miracle? What was it?

Chapter 11

The Widow's Mite: Small Coins from a Big Heart

by the Coins

I am a coin. Over the years, people have called my sister and me "mites." Do you know what a mite is? It's a very tiny bug. Because we are such tiny coins, we, too, are called mites.

You couldn't buy anything with us now, because now you need dollars or quarters or credit cards to buy things. You could use us when Jesus lived in Israel, some two thousand years ago. Even then, we bought very little: maybe a piece of bread or a bit of cooking oil.

Yet we were treasured and carefully saved by an old woman. She was a poor widow whose husband had died many years before. There used to be more of us, but she had spent the others on food and shelter. On the day we will never forget, only two of us were left.

Have you ever had a really special blanket or a favorite stuffed animal? Something that makes you feel safe in the middle of the night or comforts you when you're sad? Something that you could not bear to part with?

That's how the widow felt about us. We knew she wouldn't let us go.

◦ ◦ ◦

Back then, husbands provided the money their wives and children needed to live. When they died, that income dried up. If there were no grown children, widows were often left alone to fend for themselves. Sometimes widows didn't even have a place to live and had to sleep outside.

That's why we coins were so special to her. Carrying us in a soft bag around her neck, she took us everywhere. We were her security. With us, there was always a bit of protection, a bit of money with which to buy food. With us, she would not starve.

The widow was a woman of great heart. Crippled and stooped over, she always did what she could for others: sharing a piece of bread, watching children while their mothers rested, wiping the brow of a sick friend. She was old and tired. Yet she never stopped caring for the needy people of our city.

◦ ◦ ◦

One bright morning she walked to the temple in Jerusalem. (Christians pray in churches; Jews pray in temples.) On her way, she paused at almost every doorway, touching the doorframe and saying a prayer or blessing.

At one we heard her say, "Keep this family safe; their children are so small."

At a storefront she whispered, "Help this grocer to be forgiving of those who cannot pay."

And at a small house: "Send a friend to this old man today so that he will not be so lonely."

Finally she reached the temple, the place of worship for the Jewish people. Stunning in its workmanship, the temple stood higher than anything else in Jerusalem. From there one could see the whole city and much of the surrounding countryside.

Wide steps led up to the entrance, not easy for a woman so aged to climb. One by one she took the steps, then she washed off in one of three pools inside the door. Going to the temple for Jews is like going to church for Christians. You want to be clean.

Down she went, on a long and dimly lit staircase to her next stop: the Court of Gentiles. Everyone was invited to this hall, even if they were not Jewish. White marble pillars held up the roof, and many languages from around the world filled the air. Beggars asked for money. Sick people asked for healing.

Still her small feet kept going to reach the actual temple itself. Three walkways opened in front of her, and she entered the Court of Women. Thirteen large jars stood around the room. There, women of faith would drop in money to support the work of the temple. Because of their generosity, and that of the men in other rooms, the temple grew and was cared for. The poor were helped, supplies for worship were bought, and the walls stayed strong.

She sighed, for it had been a long walk. And then she reached for us, her feet planted firmly before one of the jars. Clutching us to her heart before opening her palm, she smiled ever so slightly.

"There are others who can use this money more than me," she said. And then she flung us into the jar. We were so small that we barely made a sound.

Lying there on top of bigger coins, we were stunned. How could we have meant so much to her and then be thrown away like worthless cast-offs?

And then a voice from the courtyard rang out.

"The plain truth is that this widow has given by far the largest offering today. All these others made offerings that they'll never miss. She gave extravagantly what she couldn't afford—she gave her all!"

Jesus was speaking, and suddenly we understood. This wasn't about the widow or about us. It was about God and taking care of others. She wasn't worried about herself. She knew that God would provide. Even though she had so little, she didn't want others to worry about where they would sleep that night or if they would be able to feed their children. So she gave everything she had.

✿ ❀ ✿

Since that day, we've traveled widely—from hand to hand, store to store, pocket to pocket. Like the widow, our work is

not yet done. If someone needs to buy a loaf of bread, we'll do our best. If someone needs a blanket to stay warm, we're on it. We can't do everything, but that's not the way it works with God. We do what we can. God does the rest.

From the Bible

Just then Jesus looked up and saw the rich people dropping offerings in the collection plate. Then he saw a poor widow put in two pennies. He said, "The plain truth is that this widow has given by far the largest offering today. All these others made offerings that they'll never miss; she gave extravagantly what she couldn't afford—she gave her all!"

— Luke 21:1-4

For Children

- God was happy when the widow helped by giving her last two coins. When have you given money to help others? How did it make you feel? How did it help them?

- Why does God care so much about what we do with our money?

- What are some other ways you can help, in addition to giving money?

For Adults

It has long been the work of the church to help those in need and to keep church buildings in good repair so that soup kitchens might be hosted, choirs might sing, and children have a place to learn the faith. How are you demonstrating gracious giving, both in and outside of church? How might you teach your children the connection between helping others and God's love?

God hopes that we will share both time and treasure with those less fortunate. Besides philanthropy—and the widow was one of the greatest philanthropists of all time—how do you involve children in visiting the sick, feeding the poor, and clothing the naked?

Chapter 12

Paul and the Fortune-Telling Girl

by the Golden Eagle

*D*on't, I thought. *Don't say anything more.*

Swooping down from high in the sky, I could see and hear the tattered girl following the man she called Paul, shaking her fist and yelling at him.

"Paul, Paul, you love Jesus! You're here to tell us about Jesus! He's God's Son, and you're here to tell everyone about him!"

Day after day, she would shout at him and Silas, his companion.

"You're working for God! Tell us about faith! Tell us how God will help us!"

Annoyed, Paul would throw up his hands, tell her she must stop yelling at him, and walk the other way.

"You're here to talk about Jesus, Paul! And how he will help us!"

Shhhhh...quiet down, I thought. *Something's not right here. She doesn't seem like she's well.*

∽ ⛌ ∽

I swooped closer, although it wasn't really my business. I'm a golden eagle, after all, not a reporter. But I can see four times better than a human. You want a mouse a mile away? I'm your bird.

The girl stuck out like a sore thumb as I circled closer. Paul was getting more irritated, just like those two men who came out of their fortune-teller's tent with ropes. Wait. *ROPES??*

And then I knew. The girl was a slave. The men with ropes were forcing her to go from town to town telling fortunes, for she had a gift for sensing things, telling people what *might* happen to them in the future, though no one could know for sure. By the looks of their expensive clothes, she brought in many coins. No doubt those men kept whatever money she earned and tied her up at night with those awful ropes.

No one should own anyone! If humans could only feel what it's like to climb high in the sky and then glide and surf and throw yourself down to earth on the back of the wind and then rise up again in glory, they would understand.

My shoulders drew back. My feathers popped up, making me look like a tough lion with a beak. Seeing others mistreated makes me furious.

∽ ⛌ ∽

So angry...so angry... I prepared to zoom in and maybe even pluck someone's eyes out, but since I didn't know who yet, I just circled.

Even I could see that something was wrong with the girl. Some people are broken on the inside, and some are scarred on the outside. She was hurt on the inside. She couldn't seem to stop shouting.

Finally, after Paul finished teaching the villagers about God, he walked up to the girl. A kind look came over his face. Putting his hand up like he was stopping traffic, he said, "Be healed! May all sickness come out of you!"

Suddenly the girl became quiet and calm, and she smoothed out her worn fortune-teller clothes. Her chin lifted, and she smiled.

Paul turned to leave. But behind his back, the men grabbed the girl, marched her back to the tent, and waved customers in. She still wasn't free.

After a while, angry customers stalked out of the tent, shaking their fists.

"She can't tell fortunes! She says that only God knows the future!" said one.

"What a waste of money," said another.

"All she does is sit there and pray," said a third.

I celebrated. Paul had healed the girl, inside and out. Her manner was now calm, her mind on God. Slapping the ground with their ropes, the two slave owners let the girl go and charged after Paul and Silas. No longer could they make money off the girl—Paul had cured her! Instead, they took the holy men to the town center and had them thrown in jail.

I had to see what was happening, down in that Roman prison, the black fortress. A peace seemed to fill the sky as

I flew closer. I could hear beautiful, loud singing wafting upward, praising God. I knew the voices. They belonged to Paul and Silas, who were cheering the other prisoners with songs of hope and faith.

⁂

And then, *BAM!* It felt like giants were jumping up and down on top of the earth. The peace shattered.

All the prison doors flew open, and all the ropes and chains fell apart.

"It's an earthquake! The prisoners have all escaped!" shouted the jailor. "Everyone is gone and it's my fault! I'll surely lose my job!"

But then came a strong clear voice.

"We're not gone. Look—we're here."

It was Paul and Silas! They were still sitting in their cell, with the prison door open in front of them.

They didn't escape. "It wouldn't have been right," said Paul.

Scared and grateful, the jailor kneeled before him.

"Sir, what must I do to live a better life? What must I do so that God will be on my side?"

"Believe in Jesus," Paul said. "Believe in Jesus."

And so the jailor did, bringing his whole family to be baptized that very day.

Instead of two voices singing now there were many. Instead of scared people, calm people now gathered together, giving thanks to God for keeping them alive.

And like me, the girl was free, on the inside *and* on the outside. I didn't try to find her, though. I knew she'd be fine with God's love to guide her. Like me, she needed her freedom. Maybe that is why God brought her and Paul together, so she could find peace. Sometimes a loud voice is not such a terrible thing.

From the Bible

When her owners saw that their lucrative little business was suddenly bankrupt, they went after Paul and Silas, roughed them up and dragged them into the market square...The jail keeper threw them into the maximum security cell in the jail and clamped leg irons on them.

— ACTS 16:19, 24

For Children

- Sometimes you have to speak up when something is not right. How did the girl do that?

- How do you think she felt after Paul healed her?

- Were the men right in forcing her to tell fortunes? What does this remind you of?

For Adults

This story is all about freedom: freedom for the girl, the chance for freedom that Paul and Silas had, and the freedom the jailor had in "catching the faith." There is an old saying, "Faith cannot be taught; it must be caught." How did Paul and Silas witness to their faith so effectively? How do you witness to yours? And how might you help others who are not free?